CAROL URENA

Copyright © 2021 by Carol Urena.

All rights reserved. No part of this book may be reproduced in any form or by any electronic or mechanical means, including information storage and retrieval systems, without permission in writing from the publisher, except by reviewers, who may quote brief passages in a review.

This publication contains the opinions and ideas of its author. It is intended to provide helpful and informative material on the subjects addressed in the publication. The author and publisher specifically disclaim all responsibility for any liability, loss, or risk, personal or otherwise, which is incurred as a consequence, directly or indirectly, of the use and application of any of the contents of this book.

WRITERS REPUBLIC L.L.C.
515 Summit Ave. Unit R1
Union City, NJ 07087, USA

Website: *www.writersrepublic.com*
Hotline: *1-877-656-6838*
Email: *info@writersrepublic.com*

Ordering Information:
Quantity sales. Special discounts are available on quantity purchases by corporations, associations, and others. For details, contact the publisher at the address above.

Library of Congress Control Number:	2021910365
ISBN-13: 978-1-63728-563-3	[Paperback Edition]
978-1-63728-589-3	[Hardback Edition]
978-1-63728-564-0	[Digital Edition]

Rev. date: 07/15/2021

Dedicated to all of you

We do not always realize that words,
Sometimes no matter how simple can
Be truly inspirational. Can keep us
Going. Can be our motivation. And
Everything we might need in our lives
To move forward; to do more; to reach
For greater heights.

It all starts with the individual
The world would be
A much better place
If we were all more
Considerate of one another
For the sake of the human race

Sometimes you have to let go
Move on and keep on living
Sometimes you have to put
The best behind you
Because you're in need of more
More like what you have been giving

All that you have ever done
To someone or for someone
Might as well be forgotten
But the feelings you've aroused
In the process will always remain
Sometimes ingrained
Sometimes imprinted
In their heart and mind
All that you've ever said
Whether from your heart or not
Whether wonderful or rotten
Remember the heart and mind record
And can always hit replay
Some things cannot be taken back
Remember time cannot do over
Remember time cannot rewind

When you receive the
Things required from love
Without having to ask for them
When they fall right on your lap
Without even expecting them
Without even really looking
Attention attraction
Consideration commitment
Honesty humility
Fidelity and fervor
Don't let it go to waste
Don't ever risk losing it
Don't ever let it go
Don't decide to look any further
And until you have found it
May the search never end

So many paths to roads untaken
So many hearts that led to love forsaken
All to bring me to the very making
Of who I am without hardly ever breaking
With God as my threshold my soulmate
Though with words unspoken
My most wonderful gift
My most precious token

Be all you want to be
Do all you want to do
Be you indefinitely
For nobody else but you

You deserve to smile
You deserve to laugh
You deserve to live
Deserve to love
For a long while
You deserve to be joyful
You deserve to be happy
You deserve to experience
Deserve to feel
Love that goes on for miles
What it means to be blissful

And on a good day smile
Be thankful for
The joy that it brings
But on a bad day show
Them what you are worth
Your best Cheshire cat grin

Don't worry about what you lost
Instead think of all you have
Don't worry about what it cost
Instead think it's really not so bad
For life isn't for regrets
Instead it's about learning from mistakes
For life isn't about casting all your bets
Instead it's about knowing what's at stake

Do more say more
Give it all you think you can
Live more learn more
Do all that life demands

Sometimes it's best
Not to listen to your heart
Because it sometimes breaks
Consider not listening to your head
Sometimes it's all it takes
Think about listening to your soul
It's always worth the noise it makes

Let the light that comes from within
Shine as bright as the sun
You will see that's when life begins
That is when you've won

Have conversations with yourself
Sometimes you will see
It's what you have been after
In it there's a wealth
Sometimes it is God
Who gives the answer

Dance to the music in your heart
Live to the movie in your mind
Soar to the chapters of your soul
And from the very start
I'm sure you will actually find
Your very life never will get old

Have the courage to explore
To experience something new
You might not know
What life might have in store
What might be meant for you
What you need to grow

You will see
Sometimes you have to
Forget your past
Forget that kind
Sometimes it's how you
Have to play
You will find
Sometimes you have to
Lose your path
Lose your mind
Actually before you
Finally find your way

If you look closely
You will find magic
In the many little things
And if you really pay attention
You will find wonder
In almost everything

Think of fingerprints and footprints
How uniquely you are you
Think of stars and galaxies
That God created too
And remember that your problems
As big as you find them all
To our Lord who can resolve them
They are actually very small
And the way that you are hurting
Our God can feel it too
But try not to forget
He gave his only son for you

For loyalty is a quality
That not everyone might have
But some can be loyal to a fault
And should stop if all it does
Is make them all too very sad

There is always something
To be positive about
The sun that shines so often
Even the rain is calming too
The changing of the leaves in fall
The ocean waves that somehow call
Focus on what is good
It's what you should always do
If you really pay attention
There are many wonderful things
They really aren't few

Think twice about giving all of yourself
To people who only
Give themselves in parts
If you give yourself in full but
Get the short end of the stick
Continuing to do it isn't always smart

For tomorrow and tomorrow
We always sometimes say
When the time to take action
Is what we call today

You might think
You're broken now
And the pieces all
Feel so very real
But what good
Is living life if we
Didn't try to heal

In a world where everyone
Is trying so hard to fit in
Embrace the person that you are
Feel comfortable in your own skin

Give yourself credit you deserve it all
Don't happen to forget
From happiness to love
And if you haven't found it yet
Don't give up hope even if you fall
For you can always bet
That if you count on God above
You'll see his timing is always perfect

Train your mind
To understand that
There's no one else like you
Learn to find
That person that
Knows there's no replacing you

Remember you're a fighter
And all you've overcome
That the days will get much brighter
Life goes on for everyone

It is you who are responsible
To create happiness within you
Realizing no one else is able
To give birth to joy but you

Don't let what you're accustomed to
Stop you from trying something new
Don't think because something scares you
It's not what you're supposed to do

Find passion in the everyday
In everything you do
Accomplish it in every way
And everywhere you go

There should be
No better company
Than that of
Just your own
You should learn
To find much comfort
Even in times you
Find yourself alone

Never be too busy
That you let life
Pass you by
Always take time
For precious moments
It's truly worth the try

Sometimes it doesn't take a plan
To get from point A to point B
But if we do all that we can
Let things happen naturally
A road can open up to us
That we never thought we'd see

For you might not realize
Everyone has something special
Sometimes hidden deep inside
That someone else might need
Don't let it pass you by
For it is through such things
By what you do abide
That the world is changed
Looking deep is worth a try
God created something in you
Stop asking yourself why

For even the rose
Carries its thorns
Appreciate it
For all that it is
Some of our actions
Can induce scorn
Even the best people
Can carry this

If you don't set the stage
For what you want
For what you're looking for
You'll live your life inside a cage
Only hoping to have more

Sometimes in order to find yourself
You have to let go of what was
Appreciate what is
But be open for what is to come

The sun will always rise
To always bring a brand new day
And in it always lies
The chance to change your ways

Don't apologize for seeking
What your heart desired
What you had wanted
Accept the answers you required
For you will never have to ask
What if I had followed my heart
How would you have known
That's the most important part

We are all a little broken
And some of us a lot
The words can sometimes
Go unspoken often
Leaving us in knots
Sometimes you have to
Let a number of them out
It's not always that
You will find peace
Releasing's what it's all about

And if you're choosing
To start over
If God gave you
Another chance at life
Learn from your
Past mistakes try
Not to repeat
The same mistake twice

Sometimes you have to
Close the book on
Certain peoples lives
In order to win
In order to make due
In order for you to strive

Not everything in life
Is meant to come so easy
Trust the trials in life
Not every day is breezy
There is always
A lesson to be learned
Our quality of life
Is something that we earn

When you set a goal
Don't just stop when you
Think that it is all that
You're able to dish
Simply set another goal
The things that you are
Able might be more
Than you ever wished

Living life with intention
Always has its own rewards
But it requires comprehension
Of what you're working towards

Love your life not always
So that you do not want better
Do not really want more
But enough that it's not
About whatever
Don't stop until you're sure
Realize that it's not
About what's clever
But about what life has in store

The most beautiful things
Are not always perfect
But sometimes weathered
Through the storm
For what is wonderful
Is not always set
Sometimes have been
Somehow forlorn

Trust in God's Timing
After all it is he who
Brought you through
Trust in the silver lining
It was also meant for you

Accept people for who they are
You can either embrace them
Or push them oh so very far
But whatever you choose to do
If take them for who they are
Or not want them near you
Consider if you do move on
Think of how you'd really feel
If they happened to be gone

Some of the best things
Don't come easy
Don't let that stop you
From giving your best try
If you believe you
Can accomplish it
You will surely see how
Your self you might surprise

It's ok to stop sometimes
Breathe and take a break
Doing it is not a crime
When your sanity's at stake

There's a peace
That comes with silence
And it's necessary at times
Yet its state
Can give a countenance
That some can seem to mind

The greatest things take time
With effort patience trust
Take time to see things through
Make the effort it involves
Have the patience it takes to do
Trust the intervention is divine

We never should expect in return
The things we're not willing to give
A valuable lesson we don't always learn
Not realizing sometimes it actually is
The reasonable things we didn't earn
In this life we choose to live
That are the things that should burn
Within our hearts for what it really is

It's not up to anyone
To approve of your
Life but you
Because it's really not up
To anyone to accomplish
The things that you do

Try to find the tiny miracles
That are hidden in the everyday
For it is when you search for them
That you encounter heaven's gateway

Let the beauty of your heart
Be what defines you who
Has time for superficial things
Let it be your soul that is
What guides the things you do
You'll be surprised the joy it brings

Don't take anything for granted
We are all on borrowed time
Love the ones who love you
And life will surely amplify

For life is never perfect
It's really all up to you
To make the most of your time
There is much truth in this
If from yourself you expect
To actually choose to do
When this much you realize
Is when you begin to live

When you find something you love
You should consider it be what you do
It's not always about the currency
But more about satisfying you

You cannot see the things you feel
But no one can really take them away
They are feelings very much your own
But you know that they are very real
For they are with you every single day
Feelings are somehow in you sown
But it is only you who can reveal
When those feelings within you fray
And can shake you to the very bone
It can be worth releasing their seal
No matter who they might dismay
Still always consider your very tone
This does not mean you have to kneel

No one can know what
You are going through
Unless you let them in
And realize even then
It's not what you do
But what God can do
That is really sobering

Remember who you are
Even if it's lost inside you
No one ever comes this far
Understand this much is true
The one that our Lord
Meant for you to be
It is written in his very word
To give up now don't you agree

The truth though it can hurt
Sometimes it's what
One really needs to hear
While lies indeed can often
Soften someone up inside
It won't always keep them near

For it is sometimes
In the chaos that it is
We often find ourselves
Pushing us in a direction
That wouldn't otherwise
On its own ever find itself

Unless you take the chance
Unless you take the risk
You might miss an opportunity
To get just what it is you wish

In fact doing what is right
Doesn't always come so very easy
But in the end it is your choice
Not always choosing what is breezy

Nothing shines brighter
Than a person who can
Find the good in everything
Who loves not expecting
So much in return
Who can keep a smile
Right on their face
Knowing that that smile
So shared with others
Isn't always earned

Your power is
In the way you think
For there is so much
You cannot control
But your thoughts
Are not written in ink
You choose to keep them
Or if to them let go

There are times the very mind
Can trick us out of living
The way that our Lord intended
Giving up on the things
That were meant for us not knowing
That they never should have ended

You can love someone
And decide to simply keep
All that love right to yourself
But what you carry
They might need why choose
To keep that love up on the shelf

For when you fall
And the pieces
Just so happen to break
Learn to pick
Them all back up
It's your life that is at stake

You have to tell yourself you can
Before you even start to do it
And if you can't trust that you can
Believe that God will get you through it

And while the stars
Might hold our destiny
We are all still responsible
To be ever present
In it to partake
For actually we are
Responsible for plenty
The ones that are liable
For the effort that is spent
The will that we will make

Make sure to always reach
Past the sun and stars
Beyond the galaxies and universe
As some have set their eyes on Mars
Reach more than skies the limit
Farther than your biggest dreams
Let nothing stop you or hold you back
Let nothing negative ever intervene

Milton Keynes UK
Ingram Content Group UK Ltd.
UKHW011345250224
438379UK00001B/172